The Oak Tree

This book has been reviewed
for accuracy by

W. F. Millington, Ph.D.
Professor of Biology
Marquette University

Library of Congress Number: 78-21183

4 5 6 7 8 9 10 11 12 13 14   98 97 96 95 94 93 92 91 90 89 88

Printed in the United States of America.

Library of Congress Cataloging in Publication Data

Hogan, Paula Z
  The oak tree.

  Cover title: The life cycle of the oak tree.
  SUMMARY: Presents a simple explanation of the
life cycle of the oak tree.
  1. Oak — Juvenile literature. [1. Oak.
2. Trees] I. Craft, Kinuko II. Title.
III. Title: The life cycle of the oak tree.
QK495.F14H63   583'.976   78-21183
ISBN 0-8172-1251-5 lib. bdg.

The
OAK TREE

By Paula Z. Hogan
Illustrations by Kinuko Craft

RAINTREE CHILDRENS BOOKS
Milwaukee

 # The Oak Tree

The acorn is a nut. It grows in tiny flowers on oak trees. When fall comes, acorns drop to the ground.

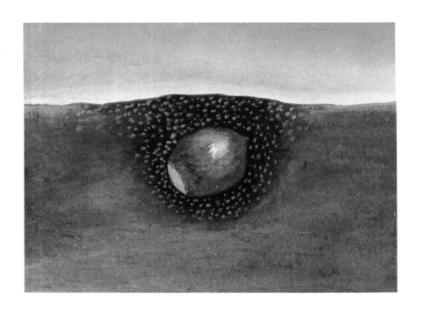

Acorns are food for animals. Squirrels bury acorns and eat them later. Often they forget to dig them up. In spring, a seedling inside the acorn begins growing into a tree.

The tip of a root splits the acorn's shell. Food from the seedling's leaves goes to the root. When the stem and new leaves fan out, the seedling starts to become a tree.

9

Oak trees grow slowly. Shoots with leaves spring from buds on the sides of stems. The stems become the tree's trunk and branches.

After many years, the oak is
full grown. Its trunk is thick and
strong. Wide leaves catch the
sunshine.

**California
black oak**   **California
white oak**   **pin oak**   **live oak**

white oak

The green in the leaves helps make food for the tree. Leaves need water, air, and sun. Food made by leaves goes to the trunk, branches, and roots.

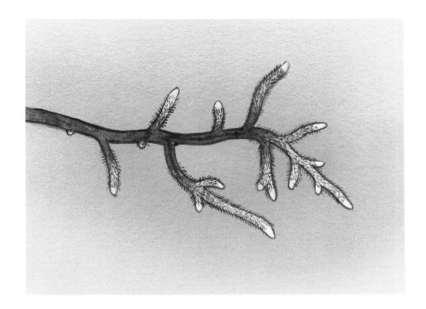

The oak's roots grow under the ground. Without roots the tree would fall over. The roots get water from the soil and food from the leaves.

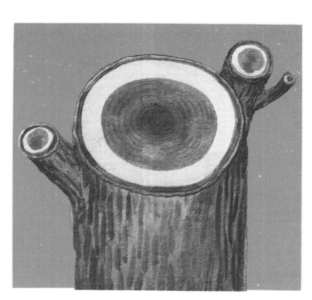

The outer bark keeps the inside of the tree damp. The inner bark carries food up and down the tree. Water goes up the widest rings inside the tree to the leaves.

Dead plants are food for worms, insects, and other living things. When animals and plants die, they become part of the soil. Their bodies make the soil better for trees to grow.

In fall when the days are shorter, oak leaves turn red. The leaves die and the wind blows them down.

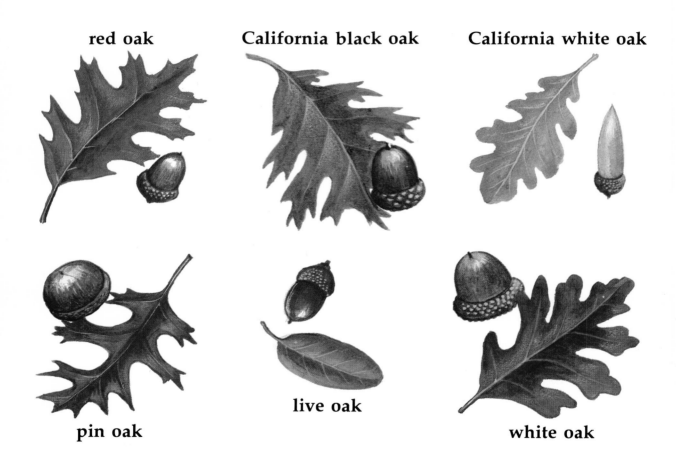

red oak

California black oak

California white oak

pin oak

live oak

white oak

Oaks do not grow in the winter. Buds on the branches wait for warm weather. In spring, new leaves and shoots come out.

Other hardwood trees share the forest with oaks. Some trees do not get enough sun. They die before they grow very tall.

hardwood forest   **softwood forest**

Pine trees and most softwood trees keep their leaves for a long time. Oak trees do not. They grow new leaves each spring. Hardwood forests and softwood forests usually grow in different places.

turkey oak

English oak

cork oak
(with bark removed)

There are many kinds of oak trees. The English oak lives for hundreds of years. Acorns on the turkey oak are fuzzy. Corks are made from the bark of the cork oak.

GLOSSARY

These words are explained the way they are used in this book. Words of more than one syllable are in parentheses. The heavy type shows which syllable is stressed.

acorn (**a**·corn) — the nut that holds the seedling from which an oak tree grows

hardwood tree (**hard**·wood tree) — trees, like the oak, that have hard wood and grow together in a forest

inner bark (**in**·ner bark) — the part of a tree's bark that carries food up and down the tree

outer bark (**out**·er bark) — the part of a tree's bark that keeps the inside of the tree damp

roots — the part of a tree that grows under the ground and keeps a tree standing

seedling (**seed**·ling) — the part of the acorn that grows into an oak tree

shoot — the small part of a tree that grows from a bud in the spring

softwood tree (**soft**·wood tree) —trees, like the pine, that have soft wood and grow together in a forest

stem — the part of a young tree that later grows to be the trunk and branches

thistle (**this**·tle) — a plant that has sharp prickles on its stem and leaves